Everyone Feels
HAPPY
Sometimes

by Cari Meister
illustrated by Damian Ward

PICTURE WINDOW BOOKS
a capstone imprint

Thanks to our adviser for his expertise:

Terry Flaherty, Ph.D., Professor of English
Minnesota State University, Mankato

Editors: Shelly Lyons and Jennifer Besel
Designer: Lori Bye
Art Director: Nathan Gassman
Production Specialist: Jane Klenk
The illustrations in this book were created digitally.

Picture Window Books
151 Good Counsel Drive
P.O. Box 669
Mankato, MN 56002-0669
877-845-8392
www.picturewindowbooks.com

Printed in the United States of America in North Mankato, Minnesota.
092009
005618CGS10

All books published by Picture Window Books
are manufactured with paper containing at least
10 percent post-consumer waste.

Library of Congress Cataloging-in-Publication Data
Meister, Cari.
Everyone feels happy sometimes / by Cari Meister ; illustrated by Damian Ward.
p. cm. - (Everyone has feelings)
Includes index.
ISBN 978-1-4048-5754-4 (library binding)
ISBN 978-1-4048-6113-8 (paperback)
1. Happiness-Juvenile literature. 2. Happiness in children-Juvenile literature.
I. Ward, Damian, 1977- II. Title.
BF723.H37M45 2010
152.4'2-dc22   2009024069

Everyone has feelings. Sometimes people feel happy. Other times people feel sad. People can feel angry or scared, too. These feelings are normal.

HAPPY

SAD

ANGRY

SCARED

There are many ways to show happiness. How can you tell when someone is happy?

Ted scores a goal! Ted is excited.

He jumps in the air.
He pumps his fist.

John plays the guitar. Ben bangs the drums. Jamie sings. The music makes them dance.

Aaron wins first place in the spelling bee.
His smile is really big. You can see almost
all of his teeth.

Rosa just had the cast taken off her arm.
Now she can go swimming.

Rosa's eyes are bright. She raises her arms and smiles.

Ping's dad fixes her scooter.
Ping gives her dad a big bear hug.

Ping jumps onto the scooter.
She zooms down the block.

Simon has finished making a robot. It really works! Simon's eyes grow wide. He is excited to show his friends.

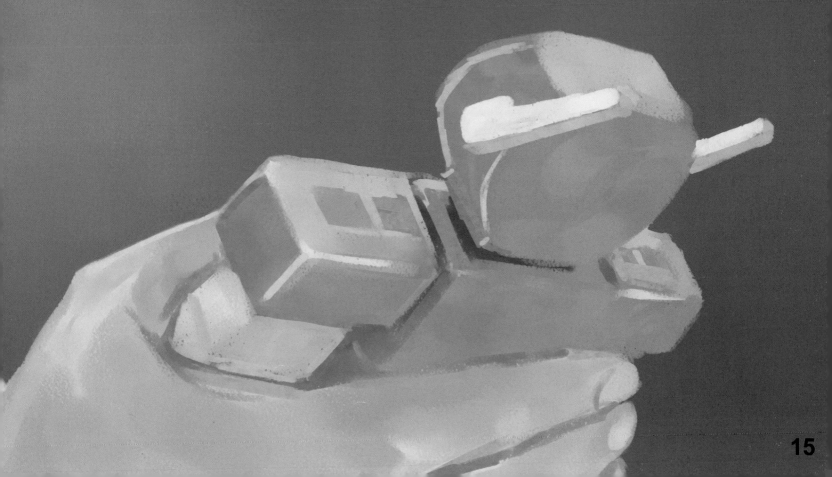

Mrs. Ross is visiting her grandkids.
She has not seen them in two years.

Mrs. Ross' eyes get watery.
She is crying because she is happy.

Lila finds a lost dog. She checks its tag.
Lila walks the dog back to its home.

"You are home!" says
the dog's owner.
Her voice is high and light.

19

Mario has been saving his money for a sled.
Now he has enough.

Mario gives his dad
a high five.

21

Gabby and her friends have a sleepover.
The girls talk and play.

They giggle and laugh.

23

Things to do when you feel happy:

- Tell your family and friends how you feel.
- Sing or dance to your favorite song.
- Take a silly picture of yourself and hang it on the refrigerator.
- Hug a friend.

Glossary

excited—feeling happy or eager

feelings—emotions; anger, sadness, and happiness are all kinds of feelings.

happy—feeling glad, pleased, or joyful

high five—a slapping of someone's hand, palm-to-palm with fingers out

More Books to Read

Medina, Sarah. *Happy*. Chicago: Heinemann Library, 2007.

Mitchell, John E. *Happy, Sad, Silly, Mad: My World Makes Me Feel*. Kansas City, Mo.: Accord, 2009.

Spinelli, Eileen. *When You Are Happy*. New York: Simon & Schuster, 2006.

Internet Sites

FactHound offers a safe, fun way to find Internet sites related to this book. All of the sites on FactHound have been researched by our staff.

Here's all you do:

Visit *www.facthound.com*

FactHound will fetch the best sites for you!

Index

crying, 17

dancing, 6

eyes, 11, 15

feeling excited, 4, 15

giving a high five, 21

hugging, 12

jumping in the air, 5

laughing, 23

pumping a fist, 5

smiling, 8, 11

sound of voice, 19

Look for all of the books in the Everyone Feels series:

Everyone Feels Angry Sometimes

Everyone Feels Happy Sometimes

Everyone Feels Sad Sometimes

Everyone Feels Scared Sometimes